REDHEADS

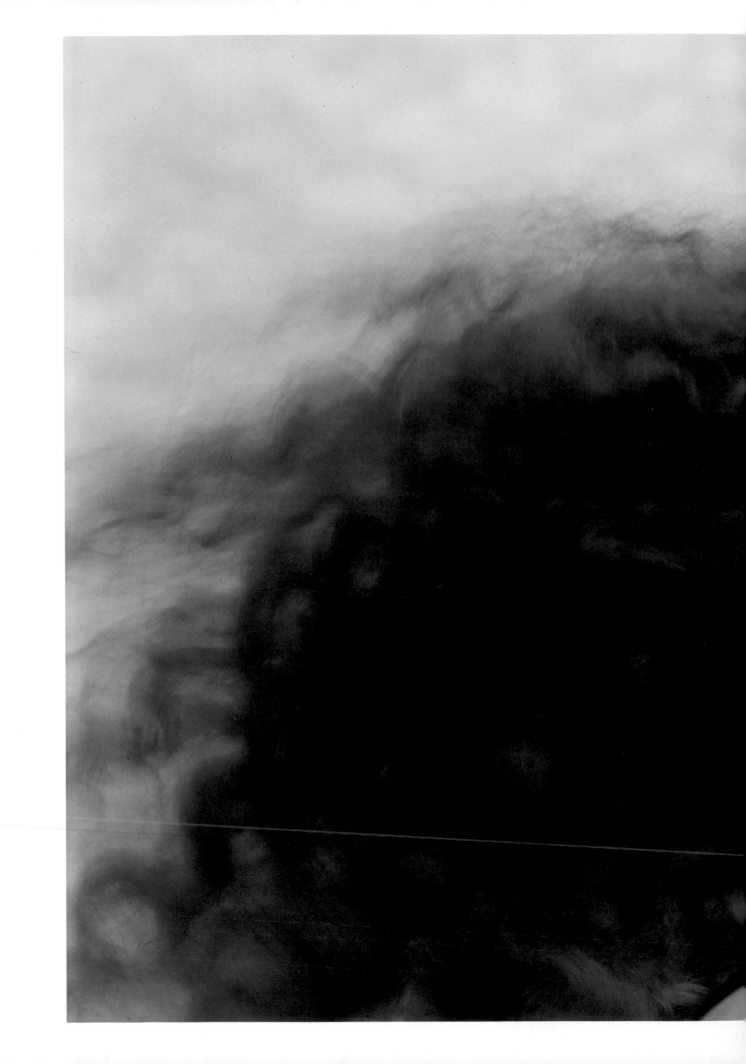

REDHEADS

JOEL MEYEROWITZ

RIZZOLI
NEW YORK

A FLOYD YEAROUT BOOK

First published in the United States of America in 1991 by
RIZZOLI INTERNATIONAL PUBLICATIONS, INC.
300 Park Avenue South, New York, New York 10010

Library of Congress Cataloging-in-Publication Data

Meyerowitz, Joel, 1938–
    Redheads / by Joel Meyerowitz.
    ISBN 0–8478–1419–X HC/ ISBN 0-8478–1451–3 PB
    1. Photography—Portraits.   2. Redheads—Pictorial works.
    3. Meyerowitz, Joel, 1938–   . I. Title.
    TR681..R44M48   1991
    779'.2'092—dc20   91–12547
                                                            CIP

A Floyd Yearout Book
Printed in Italy by Mazzucchelli, Milan
Production coordinated by Trilogy

For Ariel

BLOOD KNOT

It was always the *blueness* of the sea and the sky on Cape Cod that made me pay close attention. In this brilliance I stared at everyday items: a picket fence against the sky, clothes dancing on a line, the wind in a hammock or in rills on the water, an emerging sandbar glistening like a whale's back — their plainsong became my siren's call. As I stood before these ordinary events, I felt the sweet shiver of recognition run through me, as if I knew them from long ago. They became the subjects of portraits I made of places and things familiar but overlooked. Front porches, screen doors, an old chair facing the water, peaches on a table, a path that traces a pilgrimage to a loved place — they were all irresistible to me. My looking also brought me into contact with people, and, as I learned to appreciate their curiosity about what I was doing, I began to pay more attention to them as well as to where they lived. Then, one day, I found myself simply looking hard at someone. She seemed to be unfolding before my eyes, as sunlight radiated down and illuminated flesh and cloth. I began making portraits of people at that moment.

Bare skin in summer sunlight! That time of year when we expose ourselves most, when we put aside the mask of social distinction that clothing so often represents. I wanted to see the way skin covers our bones, how it shines or is dappled, its creases and its marks, its color, and — for the few clothes we do wear — the way they fit and feel. So my curiosity led me to an aspect of photography and a set of questions that were new to me: What is a portrait? Who is it really of? Does it tell the truth? (Does it need to tell the truth?) Whose truth? How does one go about making a portrait?

Photography quite often overturns preconceptions. In this burst of curiosity about what a portrait is and how to go about making it, I discovered that, out of a hundred or so portraits I had made during an intensive month's work some summers ago, thirty-five were of redheads. How had that happened?

Was it that Cape Cod, being close to Boston, brought out the "Boston Irish," among whom there is a disproportionate number of redheads? Or was it that in Provincetown, the easternmost destination for the summer spawn of American tourists, I found myself like a fisherman in a spot where there were lots of people and, therefore, a great abundance of redheads? I have a feeling that it was a combination of summertime, when we all expose ourselves, and of being on the Cape with that blueness of the sea and the sky that, more than anything else, drew me particularly to the flamboyant qualities of redheads. Their hair and the exotic flourish of their skin in sunlight were even redder and more visible in that blue surround. They, as we, are heliotropic — but more so. Like film itself, redheads are transformed by sunlight. It seems natural now that I would have paid attention to this new phenomenon as it rose up freshly within the larger subject of the Cape.

Photographing redheads was so compelling that I cast my net even wider. I ran an ad in the local paper, the *Provincetown Advocate*: "REMARKABLE PEOPLE! If you are a redhead or know someone who is, I'd like to make your portrait, call . . . ." They began coming to my deck, bringing with them their courage and their shyness, their curiosity and their dreams, and also their stories of what it is like to be redheaded. There were the painful remembrances of childhood, the violations of privacy — "Hey, 'Red'," "freckle face," "carrot head." They also shared with me their sense of personal victory at having overcome this early celebrity, how like giants or dwarfs or athletes they had grown into their specialness and, by surviving, had been ennobled by it. You could say that they had been baptized by their fire and that their shared experience had formed a "blood knot" among them. I had begun making portraits with the intention of photographing ordinary people. But redheads are both ordinary and special.

They are a race apart. This slender slice of the genetic pie accounts for only 2 or 3 percent of the world's population. As different as redheads are in terms of nationality and religion, they give the appearance of a strong familial connection. Were we to examine their distribution from a bird's-eye view, we would see that the greatest number of them are in northern and central Europe, the British Isles (the most numerous in Scotland—approximately 11 percent of Scots), and North America. Aside from the Yoruba, Bini, and Ibo tribes of Nigeria and some historical accounts of a tribe of redheaded warriors in Central Asia about 100 B.C., natural redheads are virtually unknown in most of the rest of the world. Of course, henna and various chemicals have done much to increase their number. Although I have succumbed to these artificial charms on occasion, I am trying here to deal with the real thing—both with redheads and with the photographic portrait.

All of us are gifted students of the human face. From infancy on, we learn to watch intensely for clues from our mothers, teachers, doctors; from our friends and lovers; from strangers; even from animals. (Haven't you caught yourself looking into the eyes of the ape at the zoo, or those of your dog, searching for a glimpse of its intelligence, thinking that with your particular powers of observation you could communicate even across species lines?)

Normally, we can read in faces love, patience, innocence, fear, understanding—the entire range of human emotion. But how emotions are expressed and where they emanate from are mysteries. Do the eyes say it all as they grow thoughtful or fierce, warm or sparkling? Or does the forehead, lined like the palm of the hand with the tracery left by curiosity, anxiety, rage, or simple good humor? Or does the mouth? We all know what charms and deceits the mouth holds. Cheeks, chins, nostrils, smile lines, dimples, each aspect of this complex organ—the face—resonates, in infinitesimal and barely discernible flickers and shadings, with the immediacy of sensation, the force of character, expressions of earthy human knowledge. Even without words being spoken, messages surge back and forth between us, as we, looking deeply, watch the electricity leap.

Asking an expression to leap onto a plane of photographic film and retain any living qualities (with any

degree of truth) is like looking into a fire and trying to see exactly which elements are being consumed as they give life to the flame. So what is a portrait? Roland Barthes has written:

> You experience a moment of fascination in the presence of another person. I cannot classify this other, the other is, precisely, unique, the singular image which has come to correspond to the speciality of my desire. The other is the figure of my truth and cannot be imprisoned in any stereotype (which is the truth of others).

"The other is the figure of my truth"! How closely that describes the passion in the act of making a photograph—that simple act, the outcome of which always leaves truth in question. The great duality of photography, which I believe is profoundly paradoxical, lies in its capacity to describe accurately what is in front of the camera—thereby signaling a truth, while simultaneously leaving us riddled with ambiguity. This duality parallels what it is like to be face to face with another person. Behind the living presence is a great unknown. This mystery is a powerful call for me to stand and face another human being, to make a portrait, to bear witness. The working question is: How do I know whom to choose?

Oddly enough, when I find myself interested in making a portrait of someone, I do not think my inspiration comes from finding an "interesting face," but rather from some visceral knowing that I cannot back away from. As I watch the human tide, I may suddenly feel a surge of energy! If I'm sensitive at that moment, I can find my way to it. Then I may see who possesses it and how it is expressed: a sense of self; a quick, light step; a moving spirit. These are all nearly ineffable sensations, but they touch me precisely.

Gathering courage, I step inside the space we reserve for privacy in the public world, and with a few words I make my needs known. The first interaction between subject and photographer contains a brief moment of originality, so one must play lightly. From my first whim the process of making the portrait begins. The two of us are already dancing. Though unlikely partners we may be, we soon come alive to the possibilities that this chance meeting encourages.

I feel that there are three transparent layers of truth to be seen at the moment of making a portrait. They overlap, creating a singular appearance, but at the same time each layer can be experienced separately. The first layer of truth is what the camera sees, the indisputable record of the actual physical fact of the person who sits for the portrait: what he or she looks like at this moment. The second layer of truth is mine. What do I perceive? I see a body coil and shift, and expressions tremble and dissolve; I wait for some signal from within to release me into action, so I can say yes to what I see. The third layer of truth is the presence behind the observable fact, the struggling human being who rises and subsides in front of the camera, like breath itself, or like the tides. I have seen that with patience and watchfulness there are moments when the three layers seem to align themselves, and it is then, in an instant, that the photograph is made. Years of working as a street photographer with a hand-held 35mm Leica have taught me to accept the gifts that instantaneous recognition offers, and, by accepting the wonder of the moment, I relax my effort to control the situation and just try to see what is there.

My method has been simple. After my initial surprise at who, this time, corresponds to "the figure of my truth," I try to establish a calm space in which we can be together, hoping that our mutual sincerity will emerge. There is no hierarchy in these photographs. Social standards of high and low, rich and poor have no place here. We are all ordinary people.

I try to follow the practice of the Japanese tea ceremony: "Give those with whom you find yourself every consideration." My only request is that each person make the effort to be comfortable and fully confront the camera. Usually, I will make only one photograph. (On rare occasions, if a fresh start is suddenly possible, I will make another.) I want to know what I feel without diluting it by making many photographs. This economy of means saves me from having an opinion, after the fact, based on superficial characteristics: "Her smile is great here, but her hair is better in this one. . . ." I am not interested in making graphic choices or performance decisions. It is either/or for me: Either the photograph resonates the truth of our moment together, or it doesn't.

Within these limitations, it is amazing to see the variations that are possible, from infants to adults, from timidity to bravery. It has been a privilege to be granted the right to come close, to stare openly. Across the space of that open stare come waves of feeling that touch upon our shared instincts in intimate and surprising ways. One cannot forget that this is a two-way trip. The acknowledgment of each other's reality is naked for a moment, and at times even erotic. By erotic I do not necessarily mean sexual, but I have no other way of describing the intensity of feeling I experience toward the other person. The strength of this connection is a powerful appeal to repeat that experience again and again, as if I could know myself from this tinder-and-flint moment.

I have stood face to face, peering in to where the "speciality of my desire" has drawn me — now, a freckled young woman, exotic as a tropical fish; here, a delicate boy nearly ready to leave boyhood, with skin as transparent as fruit; then, a little girl, half-naked, shy, but very present, whose eyes are as far apart as those of a Minoan goddess; or a girl on a path through the woods who is for a brief moment the eternal wood nymph; or a lanky teenager with spidery legs, who bubbles with life despite the scrapes on her knee. In each of them I find myself; or is it that I can lose myself, briefly, embraced as I am by their willingness, their moment of trust. I look hard. I step aside. The camera, as big as a person, takes my place. A few quiet words for heart, for steadiness. They look deeply into the lens, as in a long, private look in the bathroom mirror: It is there, in the mirror, that we expose ourselves, for just a moment, before ego overwhelms us again. If there is anything that I am looking for, it is that moment of exposure. I am not looking for a good photograph but for the freshness of experiencing life on the edge of the unknown. To get to that edge we have to sacrifice our preconceptions. For me that means making portraits without artifice: with no important look, no pretzel-like posture, no compositional strategy. I make portraits not on my hands and knees, nor high on a ladder, nor in bed with a celebrity, but eye to eye with whomever has found their way to me, young or old. I need only one or two sheets of film and the patience to see it through.

Joel Meyerowitz

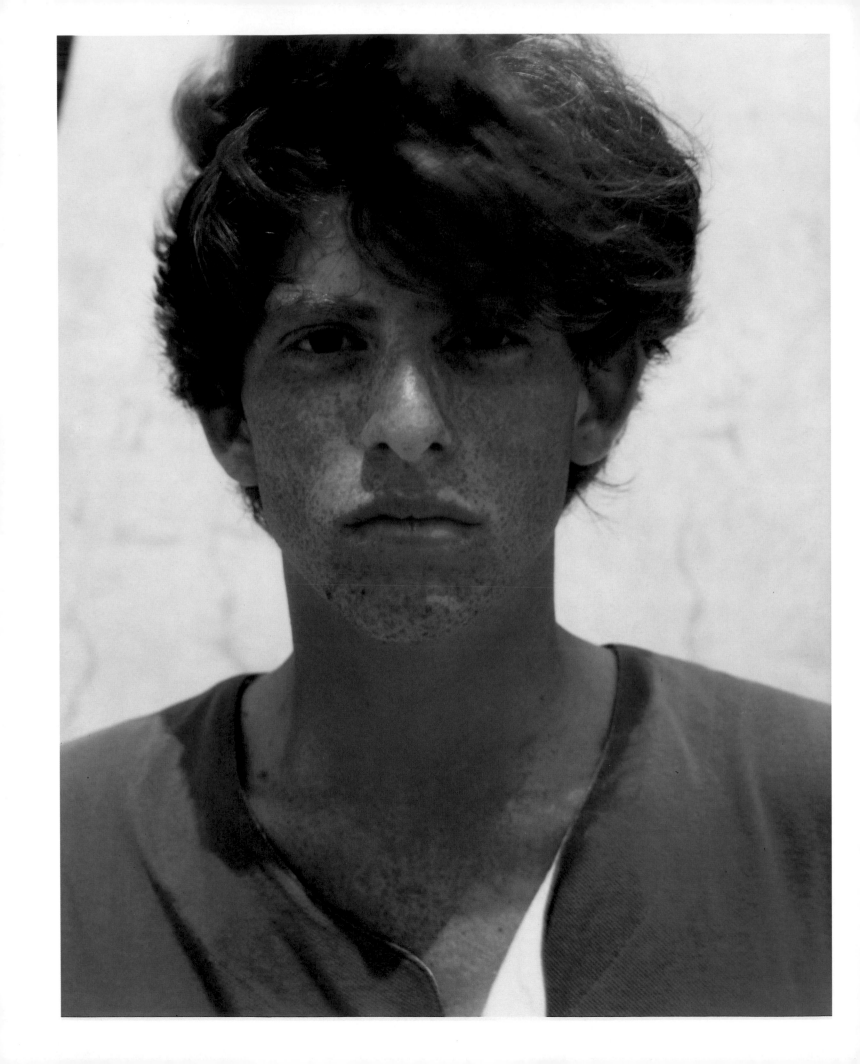

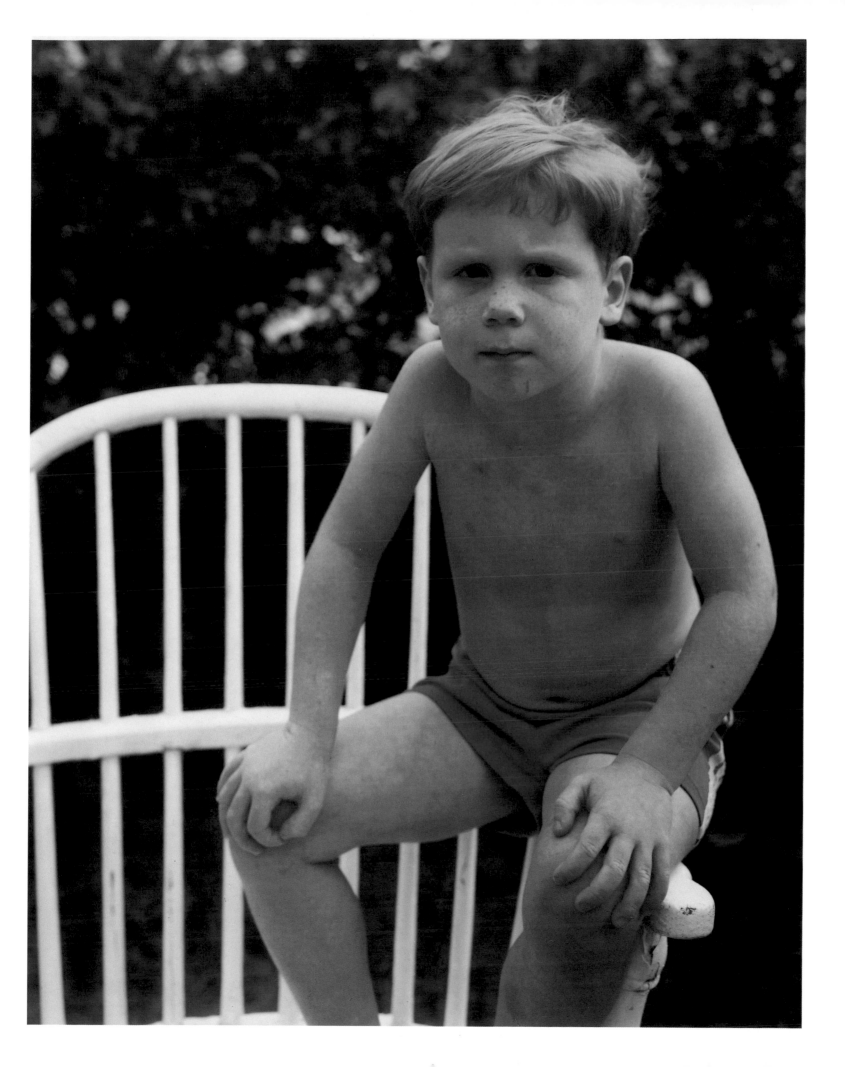